AF333260

LANDSCAPES OF LONGING

poems by

Bruce Lader

MAIN STREET RAG PUBLISHING COMPANY
CHARLOTTE, NORTH CAROLINA

Acknowledgements:

The Antigonish Review: "Behold"
Audience: "Argument to Save a Tree"
Blind Man's Rainbow: "Wedding Song"
.Cent Magazine: "Catching Shadows"
Contemporary Verse 2: "Letter to William Stafford"
Controlled Burn: "Anonymous"
The Humanist: "Attendance Check"
In Posse Review: "Idyllic Sketches"
Midnight Mind: "A Bad Boy's Complaint"
The New York Quarterly: "Our Own Blood"
Poetry Salzburg Review: "Gravity"
Solo Café: "A Brief History of Prejudice,"
    "Student Evaluation"
Thrift Poetic Arts Journal: "Promises"
Yellow Medicine Review: "Custody," "Quandary"

Against Agamemnon: War Poems anthology (Waterwood
    Press, 2009): "Agrigento, Sicily (July 17, 1943)"
Blue Arc West: An Anthology of California Poets (Tebot Bach,
    2006): "Guadalupe Field Trip"
Poetic Voices Without Borders anthology (Gival Press, 2008):
    "Jazz Funeral"

My thanks to the Helene Wurlitzer Colony where some of these poems were written, and to the College of Creative Studies at the University of California-Santa Barbara for an honorarium. Many thanks also to the caring readers in my writers' groups, and the Triangle Men's Center.

Library of Congress Control Number: 2009936246

ISBN 13: 978-1-59948-203-3

Produced in the United States of America

Main Street Rag
PO Box 690100
Charlotte, NC 28227
www.MainStreetRag.com

*For my wife, Renata, with love and deepest appreciation,
and in memory of my parents, Jack and Ruth*

CONTENTS

LANDSCAPES OF LONGING

INTERVIEWS FOLLOWING
THE SENTENCE OF SISYPHUS

VICISSITUDES OF ROMANCE

You don't want to stand in a torturer's shoes for long. Still, when it comes to seeking a truth, a certain cruelty can go a long way—right through the heart of a thing to some other side.

—Stephen Dunn

Keep death and exile daily before thine eyes, with all else that men deem terrible, but more especially Death. Then wilt thou never think a mean thought, nor covet anything beyond measure.

—Epictetus

LANDSCAPES OF LONGING

ATTENDANCE CHECK

Swapping cigarettes, jabs, chips,
they drift like Rockaway waves
from the boys home into the classroom,
ninth graders no one would bet on,
discarded by split parents.

The deck of misfortune they inherited
keeps shoving them to grow up
the hard way, hustles them
to hazardous fringes,
rips off their blooming.
A hot tide of easy dope
has begun to nettle attitudes,
submerge questioning minds.

And yet their feisty, undefeated spirits
grapple with prison sentences
of poverty; shirtless torsos
flaunt scars, coded storylines
of tested identity,
graffiti pledges of belonging.
Their dicey hands are mauled,
notched, and zigzagged from brutal
battles to breach a barbed-wire fate.

Jumpy after all-night scuffles
with gangs prowling Times Square,
they dodge and gamble to exist,
smell like a crowded gym, fists ready
for fast money, to get over
on teachers, settle scores,
stay afloat in the system chiseling them.

STUDENT EVALUATION

The teacher's a loser.
Not a scar, hands like Paris Hilton.
Believes kindness can block punches,
enemy knives that slash our blood.

He wears Disney glasses.
Never had a rival gang on his case
burning to steal everything.

Truckers, trash men, dealers
take in more money, drive cooler cars.
He should let us slide
when we don't do work,
hand out A-pluses, help even the odds.

The nerd uses Odor Eaters,
walks that snobby hood talk,
doesn't dig hip-hop,
can't get no other job.

His jokes make us cough.
No one savvies his geezer jive
like *How do you open windows
of caring and peace?*
As if riddles give respect,
could turn backstabbers into brothers.

When we're only playing,
he goes buggy, lectures on forgiveness,
bringing home the gold of freedom.
As if mushy dreams can stop
bangers from stomping.

We want the real deal who can KO,
teach us to get upmarket dinero.

CUSTODY

Suspending a minute of his daily
card game, the principal escorts in
a newbie. "Remand," he says,
"yours until his trial. Killed somebody."

Oh no, not in my class of socially
maladjusted kids, not when they're
learning to roll with the words that sting
like razors tattooing reps. Mug shots

(full-face, profile) of the fifteen-year-old
bolt in my mind; a cellblock cage
crammed with his long tossed-away time
slams in Riker's Island Prison.

The boy claims the vacant chair
next to my desk and kicks back.
Principal scoots to his office
with a view of Rockaway Beach.

"I got a gun stashed in the sand,"
the boy warns, "so don't mess."
The others caught wind of his infamy;
their noses are in the civics lesson.

I could file a grievance with the Union.
Quit. Or challenge him not to go truant,
help him hang out with books and jazz,
try to impart my bourgeois savvy.

He reaches in his ragged pants, pulls
a square of looseleaf, unfolds it. "Give me
a pencil and an envelope, show me
how to write this letter for my girlfriend."

PROMISES

We'll fly on the rooftop this weekend.
I'm going AWOL from their jail
they call a boys home. The counselors
aint nothing but wardens. Someone ratted in our dorm
so they busted me in a game of stud for cigarettes,
ripped off my allowance and grounded me.

They beat us with swat-sticks
when we don't do exactly what they order,
make us go to school across the street
where the teacher preaches at me like the judge.
He acts like he owns the world
and all I'm here to do is cause problems.
The court might as well have already convicted me
of their murder rap. If I weren't under age
they would send me up 99 long times.

I swear the pusher was pointing a gun at my bro.
I had to do something and now they've tagged me
with a bunch of absurd lies. The truth is
I've got the smarts, learned to cop my piece
of American Dream. I'll be out of here pronto
with a present to slip on your finger
and the law can't do a thing besides try to track me
down invisible streets. If they order me back

I'll just escape again and look for a job like I promised
so we can have the babies we want. I won't leave you
the way my old man left my mother turning tricks.
I'll crush his throat like an empty beer can
if I see his drunken face. But I promise
I don't want to get in any kind of trouble,
won't ever do drugs again.

A BAD BOY'S COMPLAINT

Terrified of crime
they snub glances at me
think they see the devil in the flesh
a black market of bad transfusions
a junky rapist serial murderer
another illiterate bastard
sucking dry the public tit
who deserves to be sterilized
for trafficking drugs.

After covert deals
with secret sex-partners
they drag ass back to
out of control kids in mortgaged
houses rigged Alcatraz-tight
sneak through security alarm systems
to learn about corporate scams
followed by the dawning fact
of their bankrupt lives.

NIGHT IN THE SHELTER

Hours in line to evade cold, then a scramble
for the microwave to cram in frozen dinners.
Everybody thaws. Staff guides first-timers
through forms: *Do you have next of kin? a job?*
Migrants with no English, pregnant girls,
workers who can't meet payments,
drug-abusers, daily combat-wounded
drift the vacant long aisles
in this warehouse dorm with no meals, no windows,
fold down plastic pads till 7:00 a.m.,
as I stand in fear of walking in their shoes,
eyes burning from billows of cigarette smoke.
Obvious as perfume, my name-tag announces me
a *volunteer* whose hair a provoker tries to touch.

I had thought I could make a difference to a lonely man
at year's end who might want to chat,
but find myself more alone than the Gulf War veteran
wearing camouflage fatigues in this desert.
I had imagined a teenager could use my experience,
but the boy learning con games to survive
becomes wrapped up with a racist fomenting
the mirage of an oasis loaded with hate.

To the old man groaning around a toothache,
my sympathetic comment is worth less than
an aspirin as I hand out washcloths, soap, towels.
Many get stolen, hidden in bundles
to pillow the street. I don't report the theft,
or the blood in the bathroom where men walk out
angry the water has turned icy. Others holler
the TV has broken down.

Suddenly dozens of taunts ignite a scuffle over
a trouble-maker hogging the microwave.
Someone gets a guard brandishing a truncheon.
The bivouac quiets, then reaches capacity—
five more fit on the ramshackle couches,
curl up in job classifieds. A policeman knocks,
says *Got room for one more?* A young man
straggles in with a bum leg, refuses
to go to the hospital, grits he'll be OK.

I pass him cushions and a blanket,
he drops them on the floor, stumbles
into a charity of sleep. *Lights out,*
I grab my jacket and hustle to my car,
the surprise hug one man offered
a motive redeemed in the merciless dark.

A BRIEF HISTORY OF PREJUDICE

in memory of Robert Goldstein

At the cemetery, friends remembered
the way a clique of flunkies moaned over
his comments on *Romeo and Juliet,*
how hoods chorused *Let's see your horns,*
grabbed his hat, heckled him *alien,*
sissy, weirdo freak, taunted the Dozens.
They couldn't imagine themselves
having that Frankenstein scar on his cheek.

Robert laughed them off, acted goofy,
like he owned the world. At a dance
he dared to wear the white suede shoes
punks had scuffed, swinging Lindy
like on American Bandstand with a babe
in a tight sweater other dudes would
have swapped tickets behind home plate
in Yankee Stadium for a chance to touch.

After news grapevined that Bob
was hospitalized for an emergency
hemophilia transfusion, his hidden
motive for grandstanding was obvious.
Even hoods biked with us through snow
to learn from his courage. *The bleeding*
began by itself, he shrugged, letting us
look at hideous purple-blue bruises.

Convalesced back to school, he defied
his parents and doctors, risked life-threatening
injuries to play stickball and golf,
pull wheelies and race. Sleeves rolled above
rebellious biceps, a Marlboro hanging loose
like James Dean, Bob would challenge
fast girls, persuade them into disclosing
their measurements, write them love poems.

Rocks with convertibles mooched Bobby
to read their replies, reveal sensational
details of how he went all the way.
A few wondered if the girl felt sorry
for him, though everyone whispered
rumors in school and ice-cream parlors,
realizing death would cheat him
of joys we'd know, that were his birthright.

Robert pulled alongside my '56 Fairlane
at a light and honked his Triumph cycle,
looked like Brando in *The Wild One*.
Raring to seize New York town,
he smiled and gave me the finger,
revved and revved my ambivalence
into a drag-race, till gravity dwindled
to dust and skid marks in our mirrors.

BREAKS

This pool game (the only) with my father
would be different, monopolizing Sunday
evening away from his clients' accounts.

He seemed out of practice. Three straight racks
went to me, seventeen, hands-down margins
narrowing. Then the hustler who said he hadn't

shot since his teens, said "Put your money
where your mouth is," started pocketing
combinations, my score accelerating

backwards as he bridged runs like Mosconi.
This was take-no-prisoners chess, overwhelming
offensive strategy certain as his wrestling pins

and seven-letter Scrabbles. He didn't give
an inch of allowance, targeted with sword,
I parried safeties, he gained advantage

on the table, applying subtle topspin follow
and adroit draw, manipulated me
with English. "I've seen that easy shot

missed a thousand times," he psyched
as I lined up an angle, prowled the ring
in a title bout that couldn't be stopped,

he circled and surveyed to keep the belt
and crown of his kingdom; we deployed
like rival pitchers on the battlefield

of Yankee Stadium. His legend returned,
found strike-zone corners, delivered
in extra innings like Old Reliable.

Cue chalk on nicotine-stained fingers,
he loosened collar, lit a Camel, set it
on the table-rail. Scattered the triangle.

Finessing bridge hands like Goren,
he maneuvered into position. Chips down,
a long shot balanced on the edge,

dropped. I changed the game from Straight
to Eight Ball, but he didn't leave a prayer
on the green felt; I doubled the pot

in Rotation and that shark sank winners
till I tossed in the towel, bankrupt.
"Want a rematch?" he prodded, as we left.

*

In a separate season after he died,
I puzzle out why he needed to prove himself,
fight for respect, would not be friends.

He wanted me to feel a battle he'd fought,
a child of Yiddish-speaking immigrants
growing up in a Bronx tenement without

the advantages I was wasting on billiards
bowling and girls. The merciless streets
he'd savvied didn't fancy any prima donnas,

Bruce Lader

and so you could catch worse than hell
for being an angel minding your own beeswax.
Get an iota careless and lower your guard

or neglect to keep bouncing on your toes,
you might find racetracks around eyes
set deep as a Talmudist, or brains splattered.

I wanted to flatten him, but that would have
burned like the Dodgers defeating the Yanks
in the World Series. Much stronger,

he intended to say it was absolutely copasetic
if I didn't measure up as expected,
didn't fulfill the chances he was providing

that *his* father couldn't. I would have replied
he was nonpareil, cooler than his pinochle
and horseracing buddies, a real man

who never miscued and lost control, never
messed up as a father, though the fact is
he was no contest for my scratch bowling.

I swear I wanted to kill him, and thank him
for his lasting lessons, the challenge
of transcending his proud, revenant spirit

QUANDARY

My son comes home from seventh grade
in bloody tears. Seems it started over a girl.
The bully was older and bigger he sobs.

I'm sorry he got hurt.
Should I mollycoddle that everything will be
like Gene Kelly in the phony rain?
Or throw cold water on the green-eyed flames,
say *study, do what you're supposed to do*?

Words of peace didn't prevent
low blows from punks in the ghetto I survived.
Sex was learned in the streets.
Not fighting back got kids branded
Pussy and *Traitor.* We didn't protest
like King and the Berrigan brothers,

we became soldiers refusing
to wave a white flag, warriors
the way Louis kayoed Schmeling.

Should I encourage my son to return fire,
teach that big bluffer a lesson?
One good punch in the throat or a breadbasket kick
would broadcast the message: game over.

If he doesn't fight back,
the bully will think he's scared
and keep hounding. Bullies have yes-men.
They might gang up, carry knives.

Bruce Lader

Day and night I sweat a mortgage
here in the safer suburbs. I can't manage
Hebrew school, piano, *and* martial arts lessons.

I will find time, coach him
to plant both feet, uppercut solar plexus;
he will learn the spot between the eyes
where one shot can kill.

No, a good father doesn't teach
violence is manly.
Should I order him to practice Kabbalah
like my grandfather, a rabbi?
Tolstoy, Gandhi, and Shaw were pacifists.

I would be unfair to him
if I say being tender is brave,
he'll think I'm weird, resent me
for raising a little bird.

Wiping his swollen eyes, do I second
Land enlightening words,
study like Buber, Horowitz, Malamud?

AGRIGENTO, SICILY (JULY 17, 1943)

Shells of scorched buildings
in the wake of invasion, their doorways arched
like vultures in vacant shadow flank the street.
Out of a window an unhinged shutter leans
like a coffin for Montagues and Capulets
onto one of the empty balconies barred as jail.

Men are scarcer than nylons,
no church bells ring through neighborhoods
swamped with exploded apartments.

The heat is malarial, sunlight
glares on an old woman in shawl
and long black dress, her sorrow fruitless.
Her hand extends onto a building's water pipe
for balance, like the blessing of a priest;
the other clutches a loaf of bread as she gazes
down into wreckage, uncovers
a dead body next to her black shoes.

Another survivor, a young woman nearly
camouflaged in shadow of walls,
scavenges for a meal, wanders off
carrying her fiancé's photo.

In back of them, the shadow of a Sherman tank
edges along chalky street, a shard of sky
beaches against a distant roof.

OUR OWN BLOOD

The generals deliberate on the climate of war,
insulted that some harebrained foreigners
might beat them at seizing the capital.

The generals read barometers of insiders,
tally missiles and unmanned drones.
Their temperatures escalate as the budget deficit
dives and the foreigners move forward.

The Supreme Commanders would like nothing better
than to turn the tide, reduce the expense of casualties
to zero, risk only what's necessary,
leave nothing to accident.

Fingers like rolls of million-dollar bills
toying with the buttons of boom,
the generals reckon lives,
plot exact targets via satellite surveillance.

The security of our native land hovers
like Apache helicopters
on a do-or-die sortie.

The generals know it has always been
us or the enemy, the battle between
alien blood and our own.

SCHOOL, CAUTION

The cuckoo clock strikes.
The generals stop killing time with cards,
consult CIA operatives
and investment brokers
who advise echoing their Commander in Chief.

The President salutes their heroism.
With the right strategy, the threat could develop
into the greatest war history has ever known,
might mushroom into megabucks.

The President schedules a golf trip,
orders weapons factories to turn planetary wheels,
declares it unavoidable to drop
smart bombs, liquidate the dirty deals
of hostile powers, so the world can be a place
for children to learn in peace.

Gods from glistening machines in heaven,
thousands of paratroopers obey
the chain of top-level commands,
descend like stars, fall in with regiments
to decimate the enemy, divide the spoils of evil.

In a deserted town settled with violence,
a military spokesman
denies responsibility, conveys regrets
about leveled neighborhoods,
splintered hospitals,
the collateral ruin of mangled classrooms
where children used to learn

COSTS

If they could budget a wireless security
system with infrared bullet surveillance,
they'd feel safer, it might
relieve his insomnia. He listens
to her breathing deep asleep.

A responsible step more dependable
than a dog, deadbolts, or pepper spray
to protect them from break-ins
seems as mandatory as a smoke detector.
You wake up one night and

some alien standing in the room is pointing
a gun. But the thought of keeping
a firearm handy—even a baseball bat—
disgusts them both.

In an emergency could he retrieve it
in time and feel confident, certain enough
to kill—perhaps be convicted of murdering—
someone who wasn't definitely
threatening their lives?

In a nightmare he might confuse
the woman he loves for a burglar,
or the children uncover the gun. DISASTER.
If anyone harmed them through his neglect,
he'd pray to die.

Last time he broached the matter
of the upsurge in burglaries,
reminded of the peeping Tom that police
came to chase over their backyard fence,

the vulnerable victims they might be,
she wept, wouldn't hear another word
about a gun in the house. So he
buried the key to that barbaric defense

outside the limits of their marriage.
If he gets a gun, he won't let her know.

Bruce Lader

GUADALUPE FIELD TRIP

for Robert Werling

You scan for the precise spot,
set up tripod, secure wood frame
bellows camera, fling the opaque hood
over them like a magician, step inside
the darkened cockpit, a pilot
plotting trajectory, stabilizing the hovering

condor of craft. Surveying Oceano dunes,
you balance the composition, zero-in on
trails of snake, mole, raccoon, coyote:
letters flourished across a slope,
then pull from leather bag the yellow
filter to screen out glare,
meter for a millisecond exposure
of reflected sunlight, load a negative slide.

Everything in the window is textured
contours swelling to fishbone clouds in blue.
Holding the end of cable release cord
connected to the art you depend on
for survival, a calm in the wind,
click open the shutter.

The landing area surfaces like an island
on the horizon, enlarges a chute of night
you descend to winnow the infrared
alchemy of images in developing room,
galleries, museums, studios of prints.
Collectors of light and shadow observe
sand pattern changes of perspective,
travel around the world.

HOW'S MY DRIVING?

We watched you terrorize everyone
on your school bus route—
pedestrians crossing streets
dove onto sidewalks, cars swerved
into emergency lanes. Lights changed
alertly to green when they noticed
your yellow speeding, the train
was thoughtful enough not to arrive
when you whizzed past.

Whatever you were trying
to erase from memory cells
couldn't read STOP, never saw witnesses
semaphoring wildly to slow you down.
Inescapable problems waited to tackle you,
grounded your flight from justice
with a barricade of spike strips
that made you turn
abruptly into a dead end,
undeniable proof
nobody can exceed your limit
at wallowing in booze.

Did a thought about the fifty-five
children trapped in that tunnel of torture
you steamrolled parents through
enter your missing mind?
Do you care they got delivered
home unhurt?

In case you don't recollect anything
after you've slept it off in lockup—
police video caught it all
as our panicked children
got transferred, you swore you only
had two drinks, stumbled over
the alphabet, flunked the breathalyzer.

I don't believe you will recall
failing to count backwards or forwards,
inviting the cops for chasers,
your plea-bargained misdemeanor.

So I have left this message
about the passengers kidnapped
on board your lethal weapon,
the minutes of eternity you hijacked us
hostage for ransoms of nightmare.

JAZZ FUNERAL

The crowd crescendos in Congo Square, turns up St. Peter Street,
handkerchiefs waving at
a ghost in a horse-drawn open carriage, the soul cut loose
from earthly limits
flying away free, a gleaming angel sung up to a river valley
accompanied by Kid Ory's
Creole ensemble, it rambles beyond any tempestuous
scenario of weather
to a realm where disaster and war never can be imagined.
Satchmo blowing like Gabriel
with the raggedy oddfellows moan tubas, pass Preservation Hall,
St. Louis Cathedral,
the procession of blues-wailing trombones lament a phantom
steamboat that ploughs
Basin Street to the cemetery of swamps where scattered
shells decorate gravestones,
African emblems of the bleached and watery world of the dead.

Then two Neptunian trumpet blasts herald the refugees'
return from the diaspora
to their parishes, snare drums roll spirited rhythmic flavors,
the second line lengthens
a parade of deliverance that rivers the French Quarter
with dancing Storyville
hustlers and good-time Charlies pirouetting brassy umbrellas
the colors of sunset,
celebrating jamboree the way tambourines jingle and splash
dazzling green dolphins,
marimbas and banjos dialog with jubilant clarinets and saxes,
zydeco swings in the bayous.

ARGUMENT TO SAVE A TREE

Leave that landmark alone,
it watches over our lives,
don't saw it down.

The backyard is part of your lot
by legal deed, but the tree
isn't trespassing.
It didn't intend to stand proudly
between your house and the lake,
disturbing the unbroken view
of your motorboat.

Let the tree breathe.
Building a sundeck isn't the
only way you can work on a tan,
and observe the moon
sail tranquil obsidian water.
Any otter, loon, or swan
would tell you—if you'd listen—
that the moon wants to gaze
at the tree and muse in the light
of its eternal properties.

Don't spoil that shade,
home of eagles and warblers.
From windows of loss
a friend of redolent fir
will be a missing 17-pointer.

Neighbor standing for
a snapshot on a trophy
of plundered elephantine
hulk, sawdust spurts as you
slice generations of limbs
in a minute, tornado apart
centuries of girth.

By a mountain of firewood,
you catch your breath,
light up a smoke.

THE FARM-SITTING BLUES

The heat stove's a July jam
in winter, steam billows the loft,
cloudbursts juggle rhythm on the tin roof,
a rooster bugles, geese yawp and strut.
The old black retriever tails hens
into whirlwinds, cruises the woodshop,
collars a nod in a mound of lathed
walnut shavings. I daydream

a mojo jigsaw of mistaken identity,
a melting pot of Harlem and
gutbucket blues, an "As You Like It"
mélange of Crescent City and Forest
of Arden worlds. In it everyone's
writing a lifelong chain-letter poem
with no end, gleaning inspiration
from notes discovered on trees and blogs.

Memories wander, the blues drifts me
to 1978, Newport jazz concert,
dialoguing with Dexter at the stage door
the way he bridges to his friend Francis
in "'Round Midnight," puts him wise
to the lightning ride of rambling
improvisation, diverse aerial nerves
that transmute pain into vibratos of joy

the way a hummingbird spins through
evening where frogs trombone, the calico
sacks a vole. When the friends return,
I mosey down the valley of fiddling crickets
in my clunker, a satchel of notes,
savor sets at the Blue Monk in Portland,

a cool Rogue Dead Guy, imagine soloing
tenor so good it makes the devil disappear.

Bruce Lader

LETTER TO WILLIAM STAFFORD

I've been trying your routine of writing a poem a day,
to invent an embouchure for a fountain of language,
groove rhythms of nature like breathing, produce a spring
of harmonies from essential daily tasks.

What do I know about pastoral life, a Brooklyn transplant
looking after this Willamette River farmstead for friends
east of Oakridge? Every morning, zilch; feed livestock,
goose-egg; rain tambourines the roof and my only image

is a muddy path to empty pages. Vigilant by the window
of secluded cabin, would I notice a disturbance if, on legs
of night, a grey fox skulked the distant field and looted
the chicken barn or duckling pen?

I wonder if it's possible to describe the candescent sparkle
on a crow's feathers the way Van Gogh daubed sunlight
in strands of wheat, reveal a mystery elusive as the moon
ghosting mountains of cedar and cottonwood.

This evening I thought messages were encoded in rays
filtering through the trees, and I could decipher notes of
thrush, vireo, flycatcher, woodpecker, and kinglet
intoning riffs. Were they only cabin-fever illusions

like wanting to float on a river of metaphors, compose
words for the music winding down these cascades,
the dream of mingling a waterfall of misty phrases?
Do you have a key to unlock the kaleidoscope

of light and shadow that dovetails forest haze, turns
the valley knolls into a fabric of ebbing and flowing
waves? Send a falcon with vision to decode birdsong,
a kestrel with a map of notes showing where to discover

an emerald bridge, the way you flew beyond time.

                                        Bruce Lader

INTERVIEWS FOLLOWING
THE SENTENCE OF SISYPHUS

VARIATIONS ON THE SENTENCE OF SISYPHUS

Ridged muscles of legs, buttocks, back, shoulders
strain to scale precipitous promontory, a pointless task:
reinvent the grueling cycle of his life's journey
only to shipwreck over and over.

The dead weight of night is eternal unknown,
knowledge he yearns to understand, never can
consume enough, because that colossal watermelon
remains too unwieldy, that cosmos of infinite iterations
too complex to ever grasp.

The labor perpetually derides his obsessive goal,
no access to lever and pulley,
no recourse to business consultant or computer,
no glint of hope in the soot-smeared, crepuscular sky.

And yet, he scans barren landscape, leaves no rock unturned,
remembers affairs with exotic dancers; O,
for the prospect of a diverting excursion to Monaco
or Dubai, a cedar oil massage, serene sleep,
instead of treacherous footholds on black granite.

In the dusk, his scraggy face is gradually turning
to stone, resembles a glyphic grimace on Mt. Rushmore,
feet blister to sinew of withered sunlight
as the marble millstone reaches cold crest, teeters,

the conglomerate dynasty of clay tumbles
again to canyon floor; what commandment of God
or human law did he transgress, to be doomed
like waves of salt, for parched flesh to collapse
in sand, resummon strength, ascend an ocean of effort?

ATHENA

Was justice served?
Ask the grieving wife and orphans
of the brother he knifed in betrayal.
Listen to their testimony,
report how they are living
with the verdict of unceasing labor.
Probe whether they believe the sentence
is righteous retribution for a monster
who murdered his rival to gain
the pinnacle of power, for a king
who turned his back on destitute people.
Find out if they believe the arrogant man
stole secrets from the gods
and sold them to our enemies
for ships his slaves hauled gulf
to gulf across the isthmus, ships laden
with plundered gold for building
his castle of debauchery.

XENOPHON

The truth?
An epidemic of insidious lies
proliferated, officials coined all currency
with reasons for violence.
The masses grew apathetic,
indulgent as hedonists addicted to dogma.
Witnesses terrified that goons
would revenge accusations against them,
lost their tongues.
The sea roiled blood.
Gluttonous sharks maneuvered
war machines, invented a martyr in memory
of a ridiculous fiasco.
The path of knowledge in pursuit of truth
leads to an absurd prison
of endless discontent, wagered virtue.

SIBYL

Was the evidence bona fide?
Faultless priests consulted Apollo,
the oracle spouted prophecies
like a swollen mountain stream
cascading to a fertile river valley of truth.
Orion and Sirius bisected heaven,
Arcturus ascended with the goddess of dawn.
Only death is more reliable
than the zodiac wheel soothsayers charted.
New levies loom on the horizon.
Tight-belted times approach.
Disinter the sepulchered skulls of every
innocent victim he ordered beheaded
and bronze-cast them.
He will shoulder the burden of his murders
in public spectacle over
eternal deserts of war, as a deterrent.

Bruce Lader

ANTISTHENES

A reliable source?
The scribe Polybius recorded on papyrus scroll,
undisciplined royal soldiers ransacked
our temples for gold.
Under oath, a gangster swore he witnessed
paintings of Dionysus and Heracles
ripped from walls and trampled,
debauched officers shoot craps on them.
A notorious instigator with underhanded palms
has vouched alibis for the king's puppets.
Demonic conspirators who wangled the wires
of his reign have coerced priests
into eulogies exalting the godlike bravery
of enlisted boys.
Pyrrhic epitaphs immortalize
the slaughtered, unknown, never to return.

ALEXANDER

Were there secret deals?
No one came up with a concrete clue,
while vindictive crowds relished
the murderous chance to spill
noble blood and divvy the spoils of greed.
Merciless hooligans manacled the city
with terror. The anger of Hades
imprisoned our minds.
A higher Olympian should intercede, grant clemency.
The exiled king made Corinth master of harbors
that connect Asia and Italy,
commerce prospered, common workers
had livelihoods. Odes and statues glorified
the Isthmian Games he founded; victorious athletes
received fifty dollars. He ordered the temples
of Apollo, Aphrodite, and Poseidon built.

ANGELIKA

What his reign achieved?
Prostitutes overflow our sacred temples.
Their shameless orgies with war-mongering
military officers and millionaire investors
were exceeded only by the king's
lecherous disloyalty.
Corinth is famous as the growing hub
of fornication, thanks to his regime.
He enforced devious methods to fleece
honest tradesmen, loaded the pockets of thugs
with gold. He strutted the streets,
tossing meager grains to hungry crowds,
quadrupled taxes, sowed whispers of unrest.
His eyes unseeing, ears not listening
to the infirm and elderly,
he proclaimed every foreigner our enemy.

TARPEIUS

Is the punishment severe enough?
The exercise only tones him.
Pull the loafer out of rehab,
put the screws on till he squeals the truth.
Then exile him to a scorching canyon
with mountain walls cloud-high, snow at the top.
Place hazards like gravel
and stinging ants along the gauntlet.
Every time he struggles up,
horsewhip and douse him with brine;
every time the rock tumbles and he
straggles after it, limping, trudging in sand,
remind him his wife slit her wrists
grieving their son's death in the Persian War.

MARSYAS

Is there any doubt?
He was only a parrot of priests
and military interests
who profit from the tragic suffering of others.
Envious schemers baited
then fingered him with ludicrous charges.
The majority got swept up in a surge of outcries
that didn't yield any sound evidence.
Bloodthirsty guilt disguised as furious vengeance
convicted him of murdering
the brother who had bribed fortunetellers
to drag his name through dirt.
His punishment exceeds all the gossip
and alleged wrongdoing.
The real truth spirals in the secret oracles of our hearts,
is divined in the quintessential blue coins
of the cormorant combing sea surface
to reach the sky tender forgiveness opens.

CASSANDRA

Were witnesses honorable?
A trustworthy sorceress has vouched
a slave of Sisyphus bought an aphrodisiac
from her, a confection of honey, sesame,
leeks and garlic, perfumed with fennel
for seducing his niece, a paragon of chastity.
Nonpartisan physicians found traces
of cinnamon and cloves in the hot chocolate
also used for his vile conspiracy.
He had the arrogance to transgress the river god's
No Fishing law; dozens of citizens testified
to his treason, and still he refused to confess,
didn't amend his ways an iota.
Sacred ballots were conclusive.
Even complaining Cynics and the devious
rhetoric of Sophists couldn't outweigh
solid evidence, proper morals.

AMANUESIS

Should accomplices be punished?
Chariot salesmen, generals,
urban planners, preachers,
athletes, lawyers and others,
were accessories to the terror.
Their ringleader was the arrogant
Death god, a tyrant crueler
than any mortal.
Annoyed by the fame of Sisyphus,
Hades blew up an obscure indiscretion
trivial as a ant.
Then he spread lurid rumors,
dismissed extenuating circumstances,
robbed Sisyphus of freedom,
the wife and son he loves.

THEODORA

Is he really guilty?
Five righteous aristocrats tried to testify
to his courage and good deeds.
Homer portrays him wise and prudent.
But the multilateral voice of doubt
was prohibited from voting
in the controversy, couldn't refute
trumped up indictments that weighed
less than a grain of salt.
The real culprit, the cold-blooded
monster who conspires
to stab parents in the heart
and without pity devours children is…

LEUCADIUS

Is he a scapegoat?
Of course. A beast as monstrous
as the Minotaur
must be made an example, severely punished
for the good of the nation,
so the fears of Zeus and Hades remain
instilled in our children.
We must pay our debt to the sea god,
get rid of the evil, sacrifice that animal
so rebels in the south
who've raided defenseless villages on the coast
don't plunder our inland homes.
We must defeat the heathens driven by drought
who threaten from the west,
before they steal our flocks and vineyards.
We'll conquer the expanding empires
armed for attack in the orient,
so they don't invade our grazing land.
We must never let those barbarians
who trespass northern borders
poison our minds with their ungodly ideas.

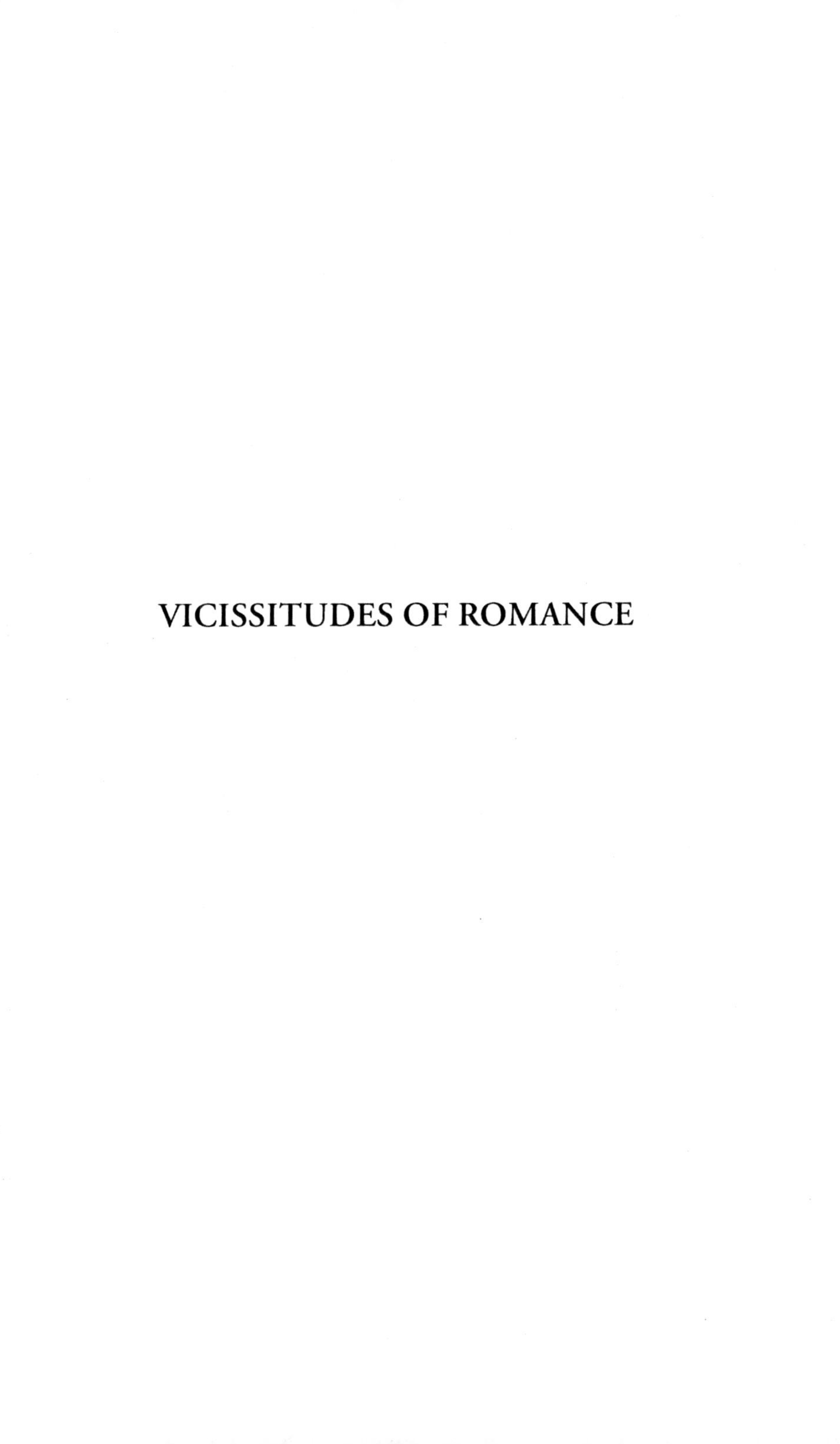

VICISSITUDES OF ROMANCE

BEHOLD

I am real,
and separate.

A mirror needs light,
I do not.

Instead
I reserve the right
not to shed my soul
as one might
remove one's clothes
before a shower,
or at the respective hour
kneel.

JIG

No
shut up
I want you
to shut up
I said No
you're not the only one
who can say No
you're not the only one

You look at me
as though I possess
the stolen Yes
like I have something
you're entitled to
some property you believe
you have the right to own

How many before
how long until
another stone
is cast into your pond?

GAMBIT

Unlike a static piece on a chessboard,
knowing his moves
isn't the same as knowing him.

The many things he doesn't speak
are not necessarily nothing;
the many things he doesn't reveal
are not necessarily missing.

Why, for him to have any rights,
must he possess her only?

Leading with a knight
instead of a pawn,
doesn't make it a new game.

ANONYMOUS

Why did it annoy him, that pet-name
"Pookie Face?" She was only endearing
her new lover. Wanting things smooth
as their massages, he thanked her
for the teddy she said looked like him

that actually looked more like his friend,
thanked her gift after closely-following gift,
felt awkward, but special, getting flowers
at work; the reversal surprised,
even excited him. It had to be only

modest exaggeration when she told him
she was like that with all her friends.
So what, if she'd also given other lovers
mini-rosebushes, still sent them greeting cards
like those he got without his name.

He would get used to the gush
of compliments that seemed
for someone else. Maybe he *did* have
a masculine jaw-line, a nose for money
and really didn't need time to himself

time he would have given her if she
hadn't gone off to stay with parents
she wouldn't let him meet, if his friend
hadn't phoned him in the desert
of vanished strokes to say they were involved.

Bruce Lader

IDYLLIC SKETCHES

1.
Reclining
she bends closer to him
under arching limbs in the shaded grass
wind ripples her unfurled hair
skirt inches up a thigh
frill of a pink slip

He is on his back
hands pillowing head
legs outstretched ankles crossed

In the march of love
it is still morning

2.
Between them is a bouquet
and candle-glow
she studies the menu
it is difficult to decide
everything looks so tempting
she slowly unwraps
a warm roll
he offers the butter
In front of him is a cocktail
and a glass of wine
he barely glances at the menu
proposes a toast
as he sips she sips
her finger uplifted in a whimsical
suggestion

Contemplating a moment
she orders the catch of the day

He studies the waitress

3.
Arriving at the door
punctual as always
he embraces her with one arm

has a surprise
behind him especially for her
in a twinkle it will be revealed
it is a time bomb

4.
Today's the big event
a thousand flowers are too few
she is busy being
fussed over in a room
he can't enter
full of sudden virgins

The gown can hardly contain her
in such a corsage of joy

at the line of scrimmage
he's pure determination and as broad
as a fullback in a tuxedo
going for the touchdown

5.
Weightless with promises
they descend the steps
float through a snowstorm
of confetti wishes
drive off in the moonlight

Other men haven't finished wanting her
Where are the women
who used to be his friends?

WEDDING SONG

Summer solstice and blackberries
   and raspberries dangle by hairs
    on exploding briars,

their many-faceted cups
   a fable of temptation
    in my careful fingertips.

I'll have dinner and wine
   ready by the time
    she returns with the bread.

And chocolate for dessert
   with these in a raku bowl,
    fresh and fragrant.

Bruce Lader

GRAVITY

Fugitives from each other,
they skulk along dark corridors
of denial, kidnap shadows
cast by a slivered moon
of eclipsed emotions.

Wordlessness betrays them
at the apogee of centrifugal flight,
as they ransom the desperate
anodyne of sex.

. . . Without a fingerprint
the tides of bodily language
have shifted elliptic;
will a touch burn or freeze?
mend or violate?
The quark of midnight:
inexorable undertow,

they treadmill between grief
and fault, looking for a vague
similitude of conjunction
nothing can rescue.

SOULMATES

They were heart and mind readers
in paradise: the studio (snug even for one)
was charming, enhanced intimacy;
perfect chemistry fixed the faucets,
afforded toasty winters, made the jalopy
the last word. But he paid mortgage
on their fantasy home anyway,
top-of-the-line accoutrements
roof to basement, singing to anyone
his love for her was limitless.
She showered attentiveness
on him, the children they wanted.

And yet they felt something
missing grow between them,
inwardly resented the cherished
offspring who siphoned their energy,
usurped their freedom and power.
They fretted monotonous daily routine,
got sick of guilt, indictments
that lacerated, scarred the children.
So he left to experience being a man.
But that wasn't enough either.
Then it was her turn to go and tell
him how it feels to be in heaven.

Bruce Lader

CATCHING SHADOWS

Knowing she doesn't want to miss
a second of the nature program
when she goes out to forage, he calls *ooh, ooh,*
>*you've got to see these spectacular shots, hurry*
as a male wildcat stalks a female in heat,
though leopard and lion prowl savannah grass.
Hurrying from the kitchen, she appears
in the Serengeti living-room, balancing a tray
loaded with dark chocolate, jam, bread, popcorn,
and he rubs it in about the rare footage: *A caracal*
>>*leaped over twelve feet high,*
>>>*snared a stork taking flight.*

   In the cut to a commercial
he grabs pajamas, changes while they watch
and she whistles at him, ribs how he missed
the clever killer whales that lurk
like shadows in breakers, till the tide rises
>and they spring out of the surf
>>on heedless seals—
>A few in the pod
>*toy with their catches,* she says, throwing
couch pillows and cushions on the carpet,
tumbling him down   *they fling the bodies*
around in sport   and tail-smack them
like volley balls   arching over a net
>*before they swallow.*

DANCE OF LONGING

The problem's gotten worse, she says
with a whisper of smile, has become
dangerous, might happen anywhere
if she gives in. At a concert or movie,
midday, even commuting home;
having caught up, it's a serious affair
out of control. A semblance of her

wants to stay with him till the video's over,
but it's around the usual time,
her eyes have been staying closed longer
than open, picturing that other guy,
that relentless inamorato.

She stretches to the surface,
a languid mermaid offering her mouth
already fevered from fathoming
kisses of a lover craving to possess her,
and the husband asks,
knowing their togetherness
an irresistible bolero,
before she floats away

in a nocturnal tide of reverie
to rendezvous with her love of oblivion,
he asks if she wants to record the rest,
and an echo—out of a mirror down the hall—
do you want her to see the rest?
makes him vanish, as they expected

Bruce Lader

from past echoes of his wanting her
to realize he is only himself,
she only *her*self. He believes she
can't do anything about the problem,
because unable to postpone
union with her paramour a moment longer

she lifts her body off the sofa
with a barely audible *good night*,
and surrendering her indulgent flesh
to his charms, rejoins his devotion,
having left, in her husband's hand,
a small green flame,
like a trace of lily-of-the-valley perfume,

and it occurs to him, as he watches the screen,
touches the remote, she is helplessly enthralled,
yearning for that meddler to entwine her
so much, she didn't suspect her husband
would choreograph this dance of desire
destined to be unfaithful.

HONEY

She plodded home from work a zombie,
so he served dinner.
Soon the washing machine
rattled like an intruder pounding down the door
and when he refused to level the load
she called him *Vicious Bastard.*

The acerbic slur stained a flagrant tattoo
in the sensitive fabric of air,
lurked like a stranger who'd murder
if you'd glance the wrong way.

Did she really believe he was
a filthy scoundrel? A reptilian reflex
to retaliate with *Bitch*
edged on heated attack, braced at breaking point,
submerged like an alligator
in turbulence before it could pounce.

It isn't horrendous enough, he thought,
that Earth is tearing at the seams,
to make matters worse
we snarl like pit bulls over a peanut.

The boulder of spite wouldn't budge.
He would not concede how his blood scalded,
never give that satisfaction.

You're no saint. You're an animal also
he justified, sniffing the scent of delicious prey,
embedding teeth into love's cruelty
as the hideous divulgence, that sweet prospect
of identity, swaggered around
like a bear, carte blanche.

TRADE-OFFS

Seeing her ebullience about the gazebo,
success with irises, orange cosmos,
dahlias and marigolds, revives his libido,

though it's difficult to say with total honesty
if the hairstyle, darkened, looks sexier
longer in back, with highlights or without,
compared to the other he thought beautiful.

He is certain the floral blouse, jazzy pants
(loose at the hip), bought for a song
in American Dream Thrift, look spectacular
as anything in Saks, or Lord & Taylor,

and convinced the matching glass-bead
necklace, earrings, and bracelet she designed
in time for their annual Valentine soiree

coordinate music of starlight. So what,
if her sitcoms and soaps don't turn him on
and she doesn't get his double entendres

or agree they add up to a lottery of laughs;
so what, if she'd rather visit Iguaçu Falls
and New Zealand. They will go there,

and to Moscow, when he partners the dances
she wishes he'd learn, the salsa, rumba,
swing, and tango millionaires tried seducing
her with, until he swept her off her feet.

Notes

The situations and personae in "Student Evaluation," "Custody," "Promises" and "A Bad Boy's Complaint" are recalled from teaching disadvantaged New York City teenagers.

"A Brief History of Prejudice" is based on the tragic life of my friend, Robert Goldstein, a hemophiliac who died when we were teenagers.

"Breaks": Willie Mosconi is the famous pool player; Old Reliable is Tommy Henrich, former New York Yankees right fielder; Charles Goren is the author of books on the card game, bridge.

"Jazz Funeral": Lines 11 and 23-24 paraphrase quotes by Louis Armstrong from an interview in which he describes the New Orleans tradition. I wanted to honor the historic city in the wake of hurricane Katrina.

Dexter Gordon is the tenor saxophonist referred to in "The Farm-Sitting Blues."

The correspondence in "Letter to William Stafford" is imaginary, though Mr. Stafford's advocacy of writing a poem a day has been widely documented.